Honeybees and Flowers

by Lola M. Schaefer

Consulting Editor: Gail Saunders-Smith, Ph.D.

Consultant: Troy Fore, Executive Director, American Beekeeping Federation

Pebble Books

an imprint of Capstone Press
Mankato, Minnesota

Pebble Books are published by Capstone Press
151 Good Counsel Drive, P.O. Box 669, Mankato, Minnesota 56002
http://www.capstone-press.com

2 3 4 5 6 7 07 06 05 04 03 02

Library of Congress Cataloging-in-Publication Data
Schaefer, Lola M., 1950–
    Honey bees and flowers / by Lola M. Schaefer.
    p. cm.—(Honey bees)
    Includes bibliographical references and index.
    Summary: Simple text and photographs introduce the role of flowers in the
lives of honey bees.
    ISBN 0-7368-0232-0 (hardcover)
    ISBN 0-7368-8203-0 (paperback)
    1. Honeybee—Behavior—Juvenile literature. 2. Insect-plant relationships—
Juvenile literature. [1. Honeybee. 2. Bees. 3. Insect-plant relationships.] I. Title.
II. Series: Schaefer, Lola M., 1950– Honey bees.
QL568.A6S282 1999
595.79′9—dc21   98-40908

Note to Parents and Teachers

The Honey Bees series supports national science standards for units on the diversity and unity of life. The series also shows that animals have features that help them live in different environments. This book describes and illustrates how honey bees collect pollen and nectar, how they pollinate flowers, and how they communicate. The photographs support early readers in understanding the text. The repetition of words and phrases helps early readers learn new words. This book also introduces early readers to subject-specific vocabulary words, which are defined in the Words to Know section. Early readers may need assistance to read some words and to use the Table of Contents, Words to Know, Read More, Internet Sites, and Index/Word List sections of the book.

Table of Contents

Honey bees visit flowers.

Honey bees gather nectar from flowers.

pollen

Honey bees gather pollen from flowers.

10

Honey bees carry pollen from flower to flower. They pollinate flowers.

Honey bees take
nectar and pollen
back to the hive.

Honey bees store nectar and pollen in honeycombs.

Honey bees dance
on the honeycomb.

The dance shows other honey bees where flowers are.

Then other honey bees
visit the flowers.

Words to Know

hive—a structure where honey bees live; thousands of honey bees live in a hive.

honeycomb—a group of wax cells built by honey bees in their hive; honey bees store pollen, nectar, honey, and eggs in the cells.

nectar—a sweet liquid that honey bees gather from flowers; nectar ripens into honey.

pollen—tiny, yellow grains in flowers; honey bees eat pollen.

pollinate—to move pollen from flower to flower; pollination helps flowers make seeds.

Read More

Crewe, Sabrina. *The Bee.* Life Cycles. Austin, Texas: Raintree Steck-Vaughn, 1997.

Gibbons, Gail. *The Honey Makers.* New York: Morrow Junior Books, 1997.

Holmes, Kevin J. *Bees.* Animals. Mankato, Minn.: Bridgestone Books, 1998.

Kalman, Bobbie. *Hooray for Beekeeping!* Hooray for Farming! New York: Crabtree Publishing, 1998.

Internet Sites

Bee Basics
http://www.roctronics.com/BEE-BASE.HTM

The Gathering
http://honeybee.com.au/Gathering.html

The Honey Expert
http://www.honey.com

Index/Word List

Word Count: 67
Early-Intervention Level: 11

Editorial Credits
Martha E. Hillman, editor; Steve Weil/Tandem Design, cover designer and
    illustrator; Kimberly Danger, photo researcher

Photo Credits
Bill Johnson, 6
John Elk III, 18
McDaniel Photography/Stephen McDaniel, 8, 12
Root Resources/B. Glass, 10
Scott Camazine, 14, 16
Scott T. Smith, 1, 4, 20
Unicorn Stock Photos/Doug Adams, cover